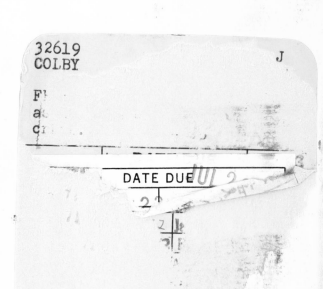

F B I

HOW THE G-MEN USE SCIENCE AS WELL AS
WEAPONS TO COMBAT CRIME

A New and Revised Edition

by C. B. COLBY

Coward-McCann, Inc.   **New York**

Contents

All photographs courtesy of Federal Bureau of Investigation

Library of Congress Catalog Card Number: 73-97609

This Is the FBI

Early on the morning of September 26, 1933, a group of armed men stealthily surrounded a small house in Memphis, Tennessee. Inside was George "Machine Gun" Kelly, formerly an inmate of Leavenworth Penitentiary, now a fugitive from the law. Quickly the men closed in around the building, crashed the doors, and charged inside with the curt order: "We are federal officers—come out with your hands up!"

The surprised and cowering fugitive, facing the guns of the government agents, raised his hands and whimpered, "Don't shoot, G-men, don't shoot!" Thus was coined a new word for our language: "G-man."

From that day on, the G-men, special agents of the Federal Bureau of Investigation, have tracked down, cornered, and either killed or captured thousands of criminal fugitives the country over. Hardly anyone living in a civilized portion of the globe has not heard of J. Edgar Hoover, the bureau's dynamic director, and the almost legendary exploits of his courageous G-men.

Their history is bright with exploits of brilliant crime investigation, and it is starred with the names of many who have particularly distinguished themselves fighting for law and order, and decency. In one year alone, nearly 19,000 federal fugitives were located and captured, many at gunpoint. It is small wonder that the G-man of the FBI has taken his place with all the other heroes of history, in the minds of young and old alike.

The FBI was founded in 1908, when Attorney General Charles Bonaparte directed that the investigations of the Department of Justice be carried out by a small group of special investigators. The following year this group was given the title of Bureau of Investigation, and later it became popularly known as the FBI, letters which stand for the Federal Bureau of Investigation.

Throughout World War I, when the Selective Service Act and the espionage laws brought new duties, the staff of the bureau grew larger, and its services expanded. In 1924 Attorney General Harlan F. Stone appointed Mr. J. Edgar Hoover, then twenty-nine years old, to be the bureau's director. From then on, the FBI took on new and important stature, and began to expand and emphasize its scientific approach to the solutions of crime. A crime-detection laboratory, second-to-none in the world of law enforcement, was established, and an academy for the training of future FBI special agents was put into operation.

At present there are 59 field offices in as many divisions of the United States and in Puerto Rico. All cases handled by these field offices are under the supervision and coordination of the headquarters in Washington, and they may deal with any of more than 180 Federal violations, ranging from bank robbery and kidnapping to espionage and treason.

The success of the FBI is based on its persistence in digging out the facts in a thorough and impartial manner — while fully respecting the rights of all persons, criminal offenders and law-abiding citizens alike. The FBI is strictly a fact-finding and fact-reporting agency. Based on the evidence gathered, and the witnesses located by the FBI, attorneys of the Department of Justice prosecute criminals in the federal courts. Nearly 97 percent of FBI cases taken to court have resulted in convictions. FBI agents work as hard to establish the innocence of the falsely accused as to help locate the guilty. Their battle against crime never ends.

Kennie Wagner, gunman and murderer of five police officers, growled after his arrest and imprisonment, "It's a mistake to break a federal law. They will hunt you down for a thousand years!" He came close to the truth.

To set down all the glories of the history of the FBI in war and in peace would take many volumes. I shall not attempt to do that here, but instead will show outstanding examples of the many important phases of the bureau's techniques, skills, equipment, and training: phases of FBI activity seldom seen by the general public.

I consider it a signal honor and particular privilege to be able, through special permission of the director of the Federal Bureau of Investigation, and the wonderful cooperation of many of the bureau's staff, to bring to you this closeup look at one of America's most important federal organizations, and the greatest crime-detection and criminal-apprehension team in the world—the Federal Bureau of Investigation under the direction of J. Edgar Hoover. I would like to dedicate this book to Mr. Hoover and to the heroic G-men, past, present, and future, who have done so much to make the United States and the FBI synonymous throughout the world with law and order.

C. B. COLBY

Command Post of the FBI

The new FBI Headquarters in Washington, D.C., is located on Pennsylvania Avenue, midway between the White House and the Capitol. Here too is the world-famous FBI Laboratory, the equally famous Identification Division, and the offices of the supervisory officials who direct and control the FBI investigative operations. To meet their responsibilities in the nation's fight against crime and subversion, the FBI's more than 16,000 employees (including 7,000 special agents, and more than 9,000 clerical, stenographic and technical assistants) must be on the job or on call twenty-four hours a day. Lights burn and communications devices chatter around the clock at the Washington headquarters building and at the many FBI field offices across the country. The G-men of the FBI never call a cease-fire against the nation's enemies.

The Director of the FBI

Perhaps no other single man in America has contributed more to the nation's security, to the fight against crime and subversion, and to the cause of honest and impartial law enforcement than J. Edgar Hoover, the FBI's famous director. Born in the District of Columbia on New Year's Day in 1895, he received Bachelor and Master of Laws degrees at George Washington University and joined the Department of Justice in 1917. He became director of the FBI in 1924 and has held that position ever since. No mere desk administrator, Mr. Hoover has been an active participant in many of the bureau's most dangerous cases, working long hours and personally directing the most important criminal and security investigations. Mr. Hoover has been honored by organizations representing many races, religions and national origins. Shortly before he reached the age of seventy, when compulsory retirement under the Federal Civil Service Retirement Act was to take effect, a special executive order was issued from the White House exempting Mr. Hoover "from compulsory retirement for age for an indefinite period of time," thus keeping him active as director. To this fine gentleman America owes a tremendous debt.

World's Largest Collection

The Identification Division of the FBI houses the largest collection of fingerprints in the world. Here can be found nearly 200,000,000 cards containing names, descriptions, fingerprints and fingerprint classifications of more than 84,000,000 men, women and children. Most of these prints have been submitted for identification in matters unrelated to any crime. The rest of the prints on file are of particular interest to law enforcement agencies across the nation. Approximately 29,000 new prints are received by the Identification Division every working day. Many of these are matched with prints already on file. Red tags on records of fugitives from justice make fast identification possible and notification of agencies seeking their arrest speedy. Thousands of fugitives are arrested through fingerprint identifications every year. Although criminals adopt new names, faces and personalities, their fingerprints never change. If their fingerprints are on file, the FBI will expose their true identity very quickly.

Fingerprints Never Lie

The millions of fingerprints in these mechanized filing cabinets can be checked through in an astonishingly short time. In the noncriminal indices are cards of prints for aliens, members of all branches of the armed services, government employees, and persons who have voluntarily and wisely sent in their prints to assure positive identification in case of death, disfigurement, or amnesia. In addition to identification of unknown victims of fires, explosions, aviation disasters and other catastrophes, the FBI has helped identify the bodies of thousands of American war casualties. One soldier's body that had been buried for over four years was positively identified by a single print taken by the FBI experts. Your fingerprints serve as a positive means of identification as long as you live, and even afterward.

PLAIN WHORL

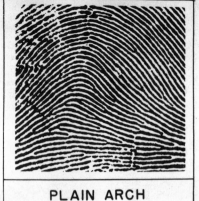

PLAIN ARCH

TENTED ARCH

LOOP

LOOP

DOUBLE LOOP

CENTRAL POCKET LOOP

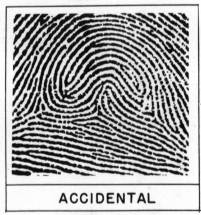

ACCIDENTAL

Which Patterns Have You?

Shown above are the eight basic patterns of fingerprints. Loop patterns are the most common, so much so, in fact, that some persons have loop patterns on all ten fingers. The second most common pattern is the plain whorl. Fingerprint cards are classified and filed according to (1) type of fingerprint pattern and (2) where (on which finger) these patterns are located. It is possible for two or more persons to have the same fingerprint classification, but upon examination by experts of the FBI, significant differences will always be revealed in the actual prints themselves, thus positively identifying the owner. Just for your own interest, get a magnifying glass, study your own fingerprints and see if you can tell which classification or patterns you "own." Look for small variations, added whorls and loops. In your fingerprint pattern you are different from everyone else, even an identical twin brother or sister.

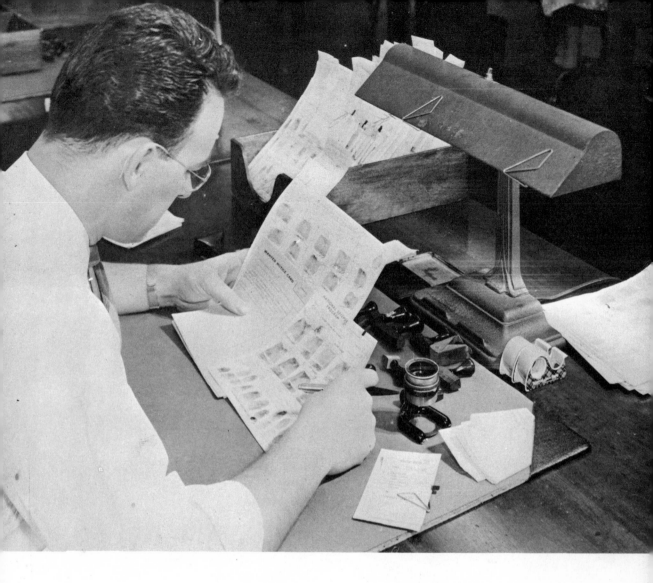

No Guesswork Permitted

Fingerprint identification is an exciting science that permits no guesswork. As a matter of fact, there is no need to guess, for often as many as forty identifying points can be found in the comparison of two prints. If the prints are from the same person, they are identical beyond any doubt. In more than one case, a criminal suspect has been proved by his prints to be completely innocent, so fingerprints can work to protect the innocent, as well as to help identify the guilty. Fingerprints begin to form about three months before birth and do not change throughout the lifetime. A serious injury to the inner skin tissue may leave a permanent scar. Otherwise, the prints always regrow exactly the same. Only amputation or complete mutilation can remove them or prevent their regrowth, and such conditions serve at once as further identification of the person involved. Above, a fingerprint identification expert is verifying an identification by checking prints against a set already on file wth the FBI.

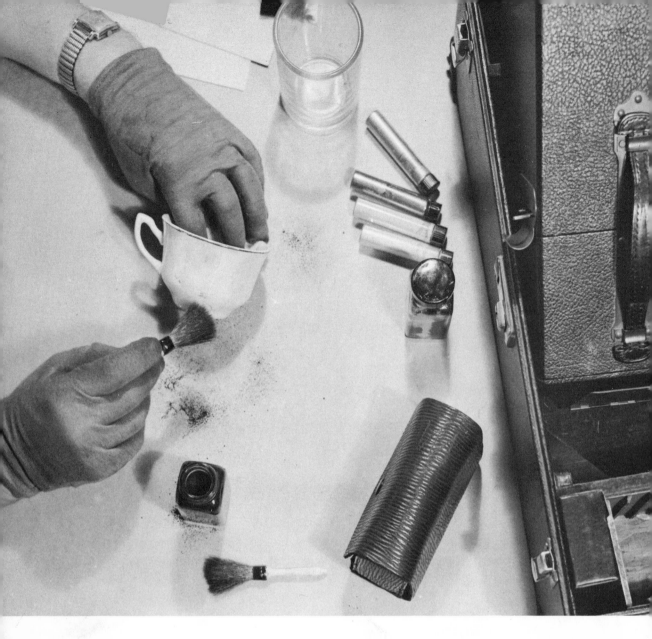

Bringing Out the Evidence

Finding, bringing out, and photographing latent (invisible) fingerprints for identification by the experts is done almost magically by the FBI agents. Shown above is a cup being brushed with black powder to bring out latent prints left by a user. The black dust clings to the slightly oily prints to contrast them with the white cup. If the surface on which there might be prints is dark, another powder, chemical or technique is used to reveal them. If they are there, they will be brought out clearly and sharply to be photographed by the special camera at the right. Bottles suspected of bearing prints are picked up by a finger down the neck to prevent smearing possible prints. Handguns are picked up by the serrated portion of the grips or sides of the trigger guard, and papers and small objects are handled with tweezers or gloves. Cups and glasses are picked up by spreading fingers inside the rim, so that no new fingerprints are added to confuse those sought by the FBI.

At Time of Disaster

When disaster strikes anywhere in the nation, the FBI joins hands with other organizations to help identify the victims. The FBI's Disaster Squad, a team of specially trained and equipped experts from the Identification Division, is instantly available upon request to assist in identifying victims of land, sea and air tragedies. Whenever possible, these experts attempt to identify victims through fingerprints, but they are also skilled in identification by dental plates, jewelry, tattoos, scars and birthmarks, as well as by general physical characteristics. Above, two members of the Disaster Squad are shown working on the personal belongings recovered from a disaster which claimed about 100 lives. Note the official white uniforms and black work uniform caps bearing the FBI identification. Members of the Disaster Squad use many kinds of special equipment in their often grim but humanitarian missions to help identify victims.

WANTED
BY THE FBI

F.P.C. $\frac{11 \quad M \quad 29 \quad W \quad MOO}{I \quad 32 \quad W \quad IOI \quad 13}$

GEORGE PATRICK MC KINNEY,

FBI No. 4,728,973

with aliases: JACK G. BEUTEL, JACKSON GEORGE BEUTEL, H. MISCHKIN, JAMES SINCERE, LEVI PATRICK SLAMP, "BUDDY"

UNLAWFUL FLIGHT TO AVOID PROSECUTION (BURGLARY)

Photograph taken 1949   Photograph taken 1951

George Patrick McKinney

DESCRIPTION

Age 27, born May 17, 1927, Akron, Ohio; Height, 5'11"; Weight, 165 pounds; Build, medium; Hair, brown, curly; Eyes, blue; Complexion, medium; Race, white; Nationality, American; Occupations, bank clerk, hospital orderly, laborer, cook, accountant, dispatcher; Scars and marks, operation scar right side abdomen, cut scar base of left thumb, pitted scar forehead, pitted scar right knee, vaccination scar left arm, pitted scar right elbow, small scar index finger left hand, tattoos, two birds, heart and "Orian" on upper right arm; Remarks, McKinney is reportedly proficient at golf and tennis.

CRIMINAL RECORD

McKinney has been convicted of petty theft on a Government reservation and of passing fictitious checks.

CAUTION

MC KINNEY MAY BE ARMED AND SHOULD BE CONSIDERED DANGEROUS.

A complaint was filed before a U.S. Commissioner at Los Angeles, California, on January 9, 1952, charging McKinney with violating Title 18, U.S. Code, Section 1073, in that he fled from the State of California to avoid prosecution for the crime of burglary.

PLEASE FURNISH ANY INFORMATION WHICH MAY ASSIST IN LOCATING THIS INDIVIDUAL TO THE DIRECTOR, FBI OR TO THE NEAREST DIVISION OF THE FBI AS LISTED ON THE BACK OF THIS NOTICE. FOR READY REFERENCE, THE TELEPHONE NUMBER OF THE FBI OFFICE COVERING THIS TERRITORY IS LISTED BELOW:

IDENTIFICATION
ORDER NO. 2756

JOHN EDGAR HOOVER, DIRECTOR
Federal Bureau of Investigation, Washington 25, D. C.

Orders and Flyers

Perhaps you have noticed in your local post office, or another public building, an identification order such as the one shown above, or a wanted flyer such as the one shown on the opposite page. These are issued on a continuing basis as an aid in apprehending wanted criminals. The identification order above was posted less than two weeks before this fugitive was identified from it as a gunman who had robbed a New York bank a year before. His arrest occurred when a Florida housewife saw this order in her local post office and phoned the FBI that the fugitive was working nearby under another name. He was arrested and sentenced to twenty-two years, but escaped and committed another bank robbery. A single fingerprint found in a getaway car proved to be his and he was recaptured and sentenced to another twenty-five years in prison. The man shown opposite was one of the FBI's "Ten Most Wanted Fugitives." He died in 1965 while serving more than forty years in a federal penitentiary. If you should recognize anyone on an order or a flyer, advise the nearest FBI office listed in the front of your phone book.

WANTED BY THE FBI

BANK ROBBERY; CONDITIONAL RELEASE VIOLATOR

GEORGE ZAVADA

DESCRIPTION

Born January 16, 1916, Cleveland, Ohio; Height, 5' 5"; Weight, 130 to 140 pounds; Build, medium; Hair, black; Eyes, brown; Complexion, dark; Race, white; Nationality, American; Occupations, automobile salesman, clerk-typist, hospital orderly, laborer, service station attendant, shoe repairman; Scars and marks, scar left eyebrow, scar left cheekbone, scar lower lip, scar under chin, scars on right and left knees. Remarks, may wear glasses.

CRIMINAL RECORD

Zavada has been convicted of armed robbery, assault and possession of stolen money orders.

CAUTION

ZAVADA HAS BEEN ARMED IN THE PAST AND REPORTEDLY POSSESSES SEVERAL .32 CALIBER AUTOMATIC PISTOLS. CONSIDER DANGEROUS.

National Crime Information Center

The Federal Bureau of Investigation has taken the lead in the use of electronic computers to help law enforcement agencies throughout the nation in solving crimes. An outstanding example is the National Crime Information Center, known as NCIC, which was opened in 1967. This center is a highly sophisticated computerized system which stores information about fugitives, identifiable items of criminal loot such as automobiles, firearms, and securities, and other data of special interest to law enforcement agencies. Typewriterlike devices which resemble the computer console typewriter being operated by the young lady in the photo above are located throughout the nation, so that state, county and local police can speedily obtain information from NCIC. Only a few short seconds are needed to obtain or check the name and description of a criminal suspect or the serial number of a suspected item of criminal loot. Some operations of the computers are measured in nanoseconds; one nanosecond is to a whole second what a whole second is to thirty years! This is indeed a high-speed anticrime tool!

Real-Life TV Drama

The FBI uses every scientific device known in its relentless war against subversion and espionage. Take the case of the U.S. Navy yeoman who was being paid by the Russians to furnish them with classified information regarding naval equipment and personnel. A small TV camera similar to the one shown above at left was planted in an office at the Rhode Island naval base where the suspected traitor worked. FBI agents monitored his movements via this camera and caught him in the act of removing important papers from Navy files. He was then followed from Rhode Island to a diner near New York City, where the sailor-spy was arrested as he was about to hand the Navy documents to a member of the Soviet Mission to the United Nations. The spy was convicted of conspiring to commit espionage and received a life sentence. Two members of the Soviet Mission to the United Nations who were involved in this espionage operation were declared *persona non grata* by the United States Department of State and were sent home. The large photo shows an actual photo of this traitor stealing the Navy documents as witnessed on FBI closed circuit television. Few potential criminals and traitors realize just how ingenious and efficient the FBI investigators are.

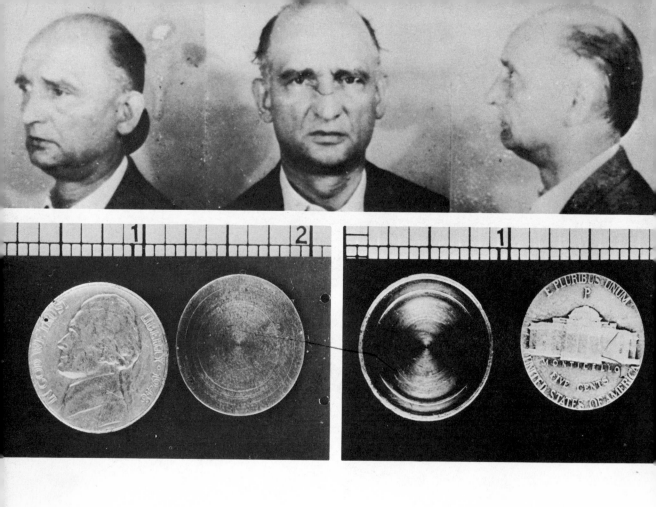

The "Five-Cent" Spy

This unimpressive-looking Russian, actually a so-called master spy, was caught and convicted, thanks to an investigation set in motion by a keen-eyed and patriotic New York newsboy. The espionage agent had been planted in America, furnished with money, and instructed to use hollowed-out items including cuff links, nails, coins, and shaving brushes for transmitting messages and orders to other members of the spy ring. All went well until one of the hollowed-out coins fell into the hands of a newspaper delivery boy and was opened to reveal a message on a bit of microfilm. The message was turned over to the FBI, and Rudolph Ivanovich Abel's days were numbered. The FBI agents found him posing as a commercial photographer and living under another name in Brooklyn, New York. Arrested and convicted as an espionage agent, he was sent to prison, but later exchanged for two Americans being held in prison in the Soviet Union. Lower photos show the hollow nickel discovered by newsboy. Note the tiny hole in the letter R in "TRUST." A pin could be thrust into this hole to open the hollow five-cent piece. On the opposite page are some of the hollowed-out items used by this high-ranking Soviet spy.

CAREFULLY HOLLOWED CONTAINERS FOR
COURIER TRANSMITTAL OF MICROFILMED
MESSAGES TO MOSCOW

WHAT THE WELL-DRESSED SPY WILL WEAR –
A HOLLOW CUFF LINK

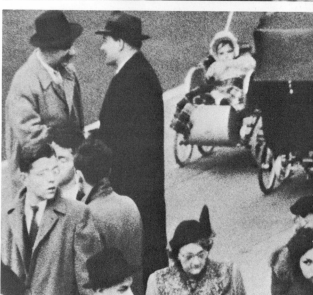

Gullible Russian Spy

In the never-ending battle against espionage the FBI uses many ingenious techniques to foil those who become traitors or those who try to make traitors out of loyal Americans. Here is a prime example of just how gullible some Russians turn out to be. In 1955 Maksim Martynov, a member of the Soviet Mission to the United Nations, attempted to recruit a retired United States Army colonel as a spy for the Soviets. Actually this loyal colonel was cooperating with the FBI. A FBI special agent disguised to look like the colonel took his place. The Russian was completely fooled and went ahead to hold a meeting with the "colonel" as shown. Upper left, the FBI "colonel" arrives by taxi for the meeting on a New York City street. Upper right, the FBI agent walks past Martynov, who pretends not to recognize him. Lower left, the "colonel" moves in to greet the Russian spy, and lower right, the Russian spy warmly greets the FBI agent, thinking he is the real colonel. The whole embarrassing mistake was photographed by expert FBI cameramen. Shortly thereafter the Department of State declared Martynov no longer welcome in America, and he left for home sadder but probably not wiser.

FBI vs. KKK

As the Federal agency primarily responsible for safeguarding America's internal security, as well as its security against subversion and espionage from beyond its borders, the FBI investigates all subversive organizations. These range from the Communist Party, through many Communist-front organizations operating under the guise of patriotic and fraternal associations, to the Ku Klux Klan, which also pretends to be patriotically American. FBI investigations have resulted in the arrest and conviction of large numbers of Klansmen for bombings, burnings, beatings and murders intended to terrorize other citizens and obstruct civil rights. The photo shows two men dressed in typical Klan regalia examining a heavy strap used to beat defenseless victims. These items were seized during an FBI investigation of Klan flogging cases which resulted in the conviction of thirty-eight Klansmen. Somehow the headgear reminds me of the duncecaps of early school days.

Scientific Crime Detection

Through the FBI Laboratory, the miracles of scientific crime detection have been made available without charge to the smallest and most remote police departments and sheriffs' offices in the United States. As a cooperative service, the FBI Laboratory will conduct examinations for any local, county or state law enforcement agency and provide expert court testimony by the experts who conducted the tests. The FBI Laboratory carries out an average of 1,000 examinations a day, seven days a week. In the photo above, an FBI Laboratory expert is shown making tests to prove or disprove the presence of poisons in fluid taken from the stomach of a murder victim. Many grim and unusual experiments and tests are conducted by the laboratory experts, all aimed at pinpointing the guilty and, in some cases, freeing the innocent.

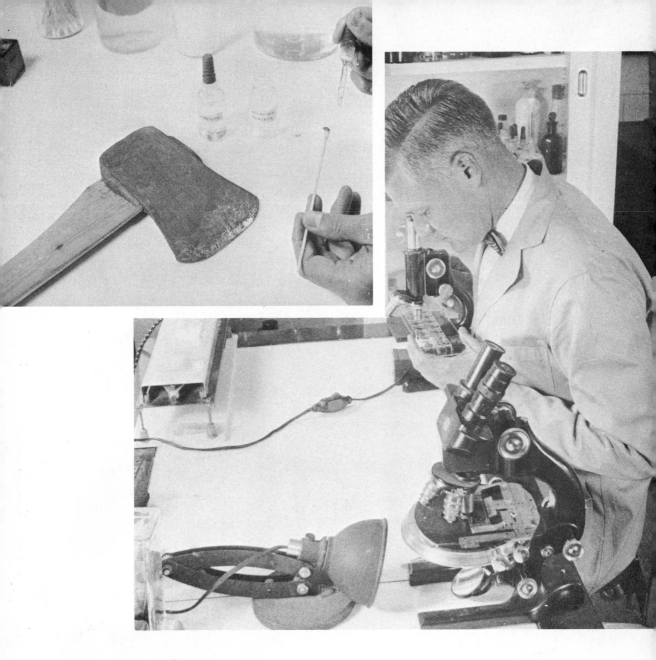

FBI Serology Unit

One of the most common kinds of evidence found at a murder scene is blood, either in quantity or in drops. The Serology Unit of the FBI is often called on to determine if a substance is blood, and, if so, whether it is human or animal blood. When a suspected stain is found, the laboratory experts go to work with complicated chemicals and techniques to give a definite report. They can tell if the blood found is the same type as that of the victim or of the murderer and if there has been a struggle. If it is not human blood they can determine if it came from a cat, dog, deer, pig, or other type of wild or domestic animal. In the above photo (left) a stain is taken from an ax believed to be a murder weapon, and in the photo (right) the serologist examines the stain to determine if it is human or animal blood. Every human has a definite type of blood (A, B, AB, or O). Knowing what your blood type is might save your life.

Conviction by a Single Hair

There are many separate units in the FBI Laboratory. One of them is the Hair and Fiber Unit, where experts identify human and animal hair, as well as various types of fibers and materials. This unit can determine if a hair found on a victim's clothing came from him or another person, whether it had been bleached or dyed, what the race of the person it came from was, from what part of the body it came, and how it was severed, pulled out, cut, or broken. If the hair is from an animal, they can tell the type of animal, and often much more. If a scrap of cloth, a rope fiber or even a single thread is found, that too can reveal a lot of information to the keen eyes and the amazing devices of this FBI team of experts. A single hair found at the scene of a crime has helped trip up more than one law violator. In the photo above, a member of this unit examines an article of clothing worn by a victim for any telltale hair, bit of fiber, or other evidence that might help identify the criminal.

Hit-and-Runners Can't Hide

Many a cowardly hit-and-run driver has left the scene of his crime confident that he will escape and never be identified. He could not be more mistaken! In the National Automotive Paint File in the FBI Laboratory are samples of paints used on all American automobiles and many foreign cars. With even a tiny fragment or smear of paint from the hit-and-run car, these wizards can determine the make, year, and often even the model of the murder car. Repainting the vehicle makes little difference. To prove this point, on one occasion the FBI experts identified a car which had been repainted seven times as the vehicle which had killed a five-year-old boy in a hit-and-run accident. Leaving the scene of an accident can result in serious consequences, particularly if there are deaths involved, and as you can see, there is really no lasting escape once the FBI enters the case with its scientific equipment and know-how.

"Talking" Tools of Crime

Almost every tool leaves its distinctive mark on the material it is applied to. In the case of burglars, safecrackers and auto thieves these telltale marks often lead to arrest and conviction as surely as fingerprints. Here an expert uses a comparison microscope to check the marking on a section of window frame against the edge of a crowbar that might have been used to jimmy the window. If it was, the evidence will be clear and positive. In the photo the FBI expert is examining several tools recovered from a man suspected of having burglarized a summer cottage, along with a section of window frame from the cottage. In the background is a small portion of the FBI's Firearms Reference Collection, which contains more than 1,000 handguns (pistols and revolvers) and more than 500 shoulder weapons (rifles, shotguns and semiautomatic weapons). These are used for various tests in cases where firearms are involved.

Comparison Confirmation

During a single year, thousands of bullet comparisons are made by the FBI Laboratory in connection with violent crimes involving firearms. As a bullet passes through the barrel of a firearm, it picks up distinctive markings on its sides which enable the experts of the FBI to identify positively the weapon from which it was fired. In addition to the barrel markings, the firing pin which detonates the cartridge or shell leaves a distinctive mark which can be traced to the weapon in which it was fired. In the upper photo a FBI technician fires a suspected crime weapon so that both bullet and case can be checked. The bullet is caught in a cotton-packed bullet recovery box so that it remains undamaged except for the telltale barrel markings. The lower photo shows a technician comparing firing pin dimple in base of a .45 automatic pistol cartridge case. In the wall cases behind the expert may be seen some of the FBI's reference firearms.

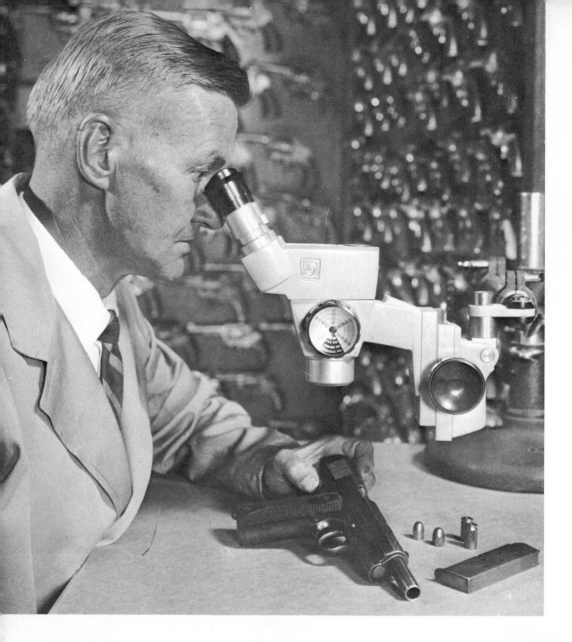

Legal "Numbers Racket"

Criminals may try to conceal their identity and avoid leaving evidence, by grinding off serial numbers from weapons they use. They are in for a real shock. Not only can the serial numbers on firearms and other metal items be restored, but they can be read and traced. Even when the metal is completely smooth and expertly refinished to look as if a serial number never were present, the FBI experts can find and restore the number. When a serial number, or other mark (trademark, proofmark, caliber mark or patent number), is stamped into metal, not only does it make an impression, but it also changes the molecular structure of the metal. Even if the mark stamped into the metal is ground off completely, the number often can be read with scientific instruments in the FBI Laboratory. Here an identification expert checks a .45-caliber automatic pistol from which the serial number has been "removed" by a criminal. Through the magic of science the number is still there to help convict him.

Shoe Prints Can Convict

Any criminal who is unfortunate enough to leave shoe prints at the scene of his crime may well consider it bad luck, for the imprint of his shoes, sneakers or boots can help prove that he was there. A plaster cast made of the imprint in the dirt or snow can be checked against a special file in the FBI Laboratory to identify the company which manufactured the shoe — or the heel or sole. If a suspect has a similar shoe, it can be sent to the laboratory for comparison with the plaster cast from the crime scene. Shown is the cast of an impression being compared with a suspect's shoe. They are matched on type of heel and sole, make and distinctive scars. Behind the technician are files containing photos of many types of heels, composition soles, etc. used for comparison and confirmation of such evidence.

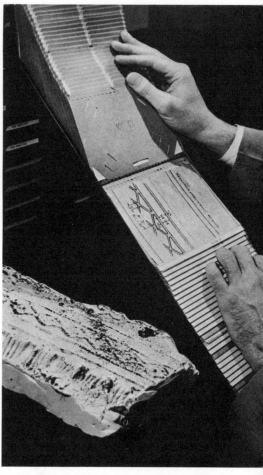

Tire Prints Also "Talk"

Even when a criminal rides to the scene of a crime in a vehicle and never gets out to leave a shoe print, he may have left his mark. In the FBI reference file of tire treads there are hundreds of diagrams of the designs appearing on various makes and styles of tires. As they travel along streets and highways, tires develop cuts, scars and other distinctive markings which may show up in a photograph or plaster cast of tread marks at a crime scene. Above, at left, is an FBI technician comparing a tire print with the tire from a suspect's car believed to have been used in a crime. At right, is shown a plaster cast of a tire mark found at a scene being checked against a similar pattern in the FBI tire-tread file. Tire prints, like shoe prints, can be valuable circumstantial evidence.

Element Detective

No matter how small a piece of evidence may be, it can still be of great importance to a criminal investigation. Even a very small particle may be enough to place a person at the scene of a crime or link him to it directly. This skilled FBI technician is operating a gamma ray spectrometer which is used to perform neutron activation analyses. This can determine not only what elements are present, even in tiny amounts, but the quantity as well. For example, it can detect tiny traces of the chemicals used in cartridge primers on the hands of a person suspected of using a firearm or, just as impartially, can show that there are no traces of the telltale substance on the suspect's hands.

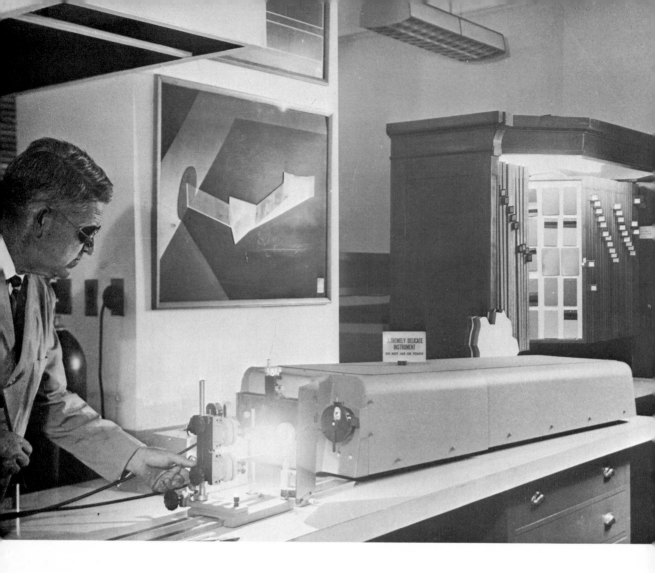

Spectrographic Examinations

When a bit of metallic substance is found on the body of a victim, or on the person of a suspect, at the scene of a crime, it may prove to be the missing link in a chain of evidence. Its nature and metallic content must be determined. These bits are burned in the spectrograph shown above so that the light given off may be split by a prism into different light waves, or wavelengths. By recording and studying these lines or waves, the exact content of the bits of metallic evidence may be determined scientifically, thus linking the victim or suspect with the crime, the place of the crime, or some other place involved. For example, if a criminal works in a cutlery plant and traces of the same type of metal used in the manufacture of cutlery are found at the scene of the crime — perhaps bits that have fallen from his shoe soles or pants' cuffs — these may help place the suspect at that scene. On the opposite page is a recording infrared spectrophotometer which is used to determine the composition of nonmetallic or organic substances. This too can help the FBI investigators complete the chain of evidence against a criminal suspect.

SLIT CONTROLS

RECORDING INFRARED SPECTROPHOTOMETER
MODEL 21   SERIAL 221
THE PERKIN-ELMER CORPORATION

PEN RESPONSE SPEED

SOURCE CONTROL

Fertile Soil

The FBI Laboratory is frequently asked to analyze soil samples or dirt found on a suspect's shoes or the tires or fenders of his vehicle. These samples may link him to the scene of a crime. These two instruments make it possible to conduct such examinations. The tall instrument in the background is the control panel of an X-ray diffractometer which can analyze crystalline materials in soil, to find out if samples have come from the same area. The instrument at the left is a differential thermal analyzer, used to tell what compounds are present in cements, clays, safe insulation and similar materials. Traces of insulation from a safe's interior found on a suspect's shoes or clothing can help prove that he is a safe burglar — since the fireproofing material used in safes is very distinctive and can be positively identified. Crime rarely pays for long, once the FBI enters the picture with its scientific laboratory equipment and skilled experts.

Documentary Proof

Every year the FBI is asked to help identify the persons who issue approximately 30,000 fraudulent checks valued at between $7,000,000 and $9,000,000. More than one-half of these are promptly identified by specimens in the FBI's mammoth National Fraudulent Check File, and almost one-half of this group of checks are identified as the handiwork of known criminals with previous FBI records. Above, an FBI expert and his assistant check the signatures on stolen money orders against those on file. Extortion letters, ransom notes, bank holdup notes, and related types of written and printed evidence are also traced to their writers by use of similar files. All kinds of documents (hand printed, handwritten, or even made from words or letters cut from publications) are examined by the FBI experts.

The Training Never Ends

From the moment that a special agent takes his oath of office, he discovers that training is a never-ending process in the FBI. His career begins with a fourteen-week training program at the FBI's facilities in Washington, D.C., and on the Marine Corps Base at Quantico, Virginia. At every field office to which he may be assigned, no matter where it is located, conferences and seminars will be conducted on a regular basis to keep him advised of changes in the FBI's procedures and authority and to help him keep abreast of new techniques and investigative equipment. Periodically every special agent must return to Washington to participate in advanced training schools dealing with kidnap investigations, civil rights cases, counterintelligence operations, etc. The special agent who is "too old to learn" new tricks is too old to serve the FBI in its fight against crime and subversion. Above is a typical training class at the FBI Headquarters in Washington.

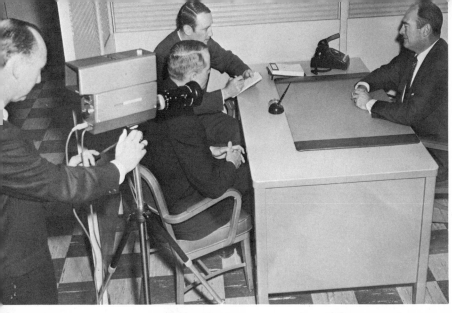

TV Helps Improve Technique

There is a special technique in interviewing victims, witnesses and others with whom the special agents come in contact. Newly appointed men are shown here conducting an interview with a "car theft victim" while other members of their training class (bottom photo) watch by closed circuit television in a nearby room. After the interview is over, the two agents will be rated by their instructor and classmates on skill in questioning, types of questions asked and (probably) some they have forgotten to ask. Use of the closed circuit TV permits an entire class to kibitz on the training interview; they can look over the shoulders of their classmates and listen without being seen themselves. This makes the practice interview a lot more realistic.

Most Robbed Bank

This is a bank robbery that is never reported to the FBI, for the simple reason the bank robbers and the tellers behind the counter all are assigned to the FBI's Training Division — some as trainees and others as staff members. This "Bank of Rangeville" is robbed almost every week as part of a realistic course in criminal investigation. The "bandits" invariably leave behind fingerprints, shoe prints, tire tracks or other items of evidence that the trainees have to spot, identify and then fit into their investigation and solution of the holdup. All types of hypothetical crimes are set up as realistically as possible, to give the trainees the most accurate situations and circumstances in which to put their training to use. Learning by doing gives better training than just reading from a book or listening to lectures, and the techniques learned are better remembered by the trainees.

Smoking Out the Criminals

Shown here is another practice exercise the special agent trainees take part in during their fourteen-week training period. The problem is to raid a "criminal hideout" in which FBI instructors have holed up to see how the trainees will get them out. They can, and do, use every trick in the book to avoid "arrest." Here the criminals have used their own smoke bomb to keep the rookies out of the building, but the well-trained students have donned gas masks and have simply waited for the smoke to drive the instructor-criminals out into their waiting handcuffs. In other practice problems the student G-men are shown how to set up roadblocks and how to search fields or forests where gunmen are believed to be hiding. Such training can result in quick and efficient apprehension of fugitive criminals with a minimum of danger to the criminals, the special agents and bystanders.

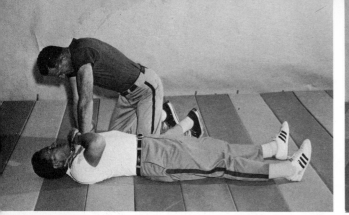

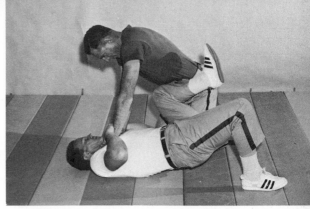

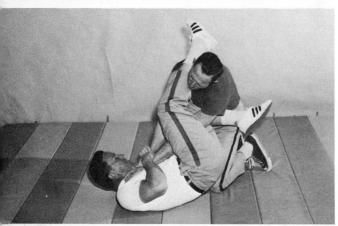

Never Tangle with a Special Agent

Every special agent of the FBI not only is a skilled marksman with many different types of weapons, but is trained in the art of defense against physical attack as well. The training program for special agents molds skills associated with boxing, wrestling, judo, jujitsu, and even football into one effective and simple defensive system all trainees master. Here we see a special agent apparently at the mercy of a "criminal" who has him by the throat. By following the photos left to right, top to bottom, you can see the simple and effective way in which the "victim" becomes the captor in about two seconds. Many special agents are former athletes, and all keep in top physical condition as many an unsuspecting criminal has discovered to his black-and-blue regret.

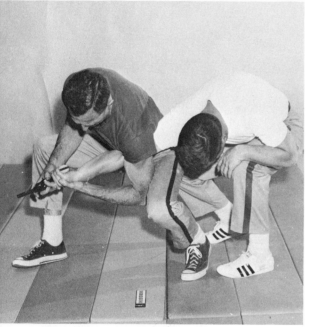

Disarming a Gunman

All special agents know what to do when confronted by an armed assailant and how to do it quickly and effectively. In the above photos, left to right and top to bottom, is shown one method of disarming a criminal who points a gun at an agent at close range. Like all defensive techniques taught the special agents, the method is deceptively simple when performed by experts, yet requires split-second timing and long training. Just as no one should ever play with a firearm or other weapon, such disarming tactics should never be attempted as a trick or a joke on another person, for they can result in serious or even fatal injury. Even though the training is carried out by experts in top condition, special floor mats and "dummy" weapons are used to safeguard against injury.

.38-Caliber Marksmen

Every special agent is taught the expert use of the .38-caliber revolver, the official weapon which the FBI issues to its men. Some are already familiar with firearms while others have never fired a weapon before; all are experts by the time they have completed the weapons course. First they are taught the safety rules and then how to use their weapons with blinding speed and accuracy. Every FBI agent must be able to draw his weapon rapidly from the holster, and consistently hit a man-sized silhouette target at 21 feet. G-men never draw their weapons to fire unless in deadly earnest, but when they do, there are no finer marksmen.

Practical Pistol Course

This course is designed to give FBI special agents practical experience in pistol shooting from all positions, at various distances, under all conditions that might be encountered under actual combat conditions. On this course, the men are required to fire fifty shots into a silhouette target in six minutes ten seconds. The first ten must be fired within twenty-five seconds (including reloading of weapon after first five shots) from the hip at 7 yards. Five more are fired prone from 60 yards. Twenty are fired from 50 yards: five sitting, five prone, five with the left hand and five with the right hand, while standing behind a barricade. Five more are fired from a kneeling position at 25 yards, and finally five with each hand from behind a barricade 25 yards from the target. The highest score possible is 100 points and many agents belong to the "Possible Club." The average score of FBI agents is over 90 points and the minimum qualifying score is 60. (The author, invited to fire the course, squeaked by with a 63.) Photos show various positions and distances required on PPC, as the course is known.

Foe or Friend?

In the deadly business of stopping armed and desperate criminals or perhaps a deranged gunman gone beserk amid innocent bystanders, law enforcement officers must be able to determine when to shoot to kill and when to hold their fire. On the FBI range, exercises are carried out to help agents make such decisions in a split second. G-men learn to use the powerful slug fired from a repeating shotgun. In the top photo a trainee is shown firing these heavy slugs at silhouette targets. He is expected to bring down five targets with five shots. In the lower photo we see a section of "Hogan's Alley," where life-size figures appear in doors and windows as the trainee walks past. Some are armed with deadly weapons while others are unarmed citizens. The agent must draw his revolver and make an instant decision on whether to fire or not. Note figure of man in barbershop doorway.

Famous FBI Fast Draw

In these six photos the special agent's world-famous "fast draw" is shown. G-men are instructed to shoot only in defense of their own or another person's life. They shoot to kill, not to warn or wound, because it is the philosophy of the FBI that: "The person who is not justified in killing is not justified in shooting at all." This series of stop-action high-speed photos shows the draw from first position with hands at side and coat unbuttoned to last position with revolver in firing position. This takes less than a second when done by the highly trained men of the Federal Bureau of Investigation. The special agents have to keep in training for all types of defensive tactics and marksmanship, as well as this fast draw. Their own lives, the lives of other agents and of innocent bystanders depend on such skills.

Powerful Weapon Against Crime

When fired by the expert marksmen of the FBI, the Thompson submachine gun is one of the most effective weapons for law and order. Firing at the rate of 600 shots a minute on "full automatic," the tommy gun can stop any fugitive in a hail of .45-caliber bullets. The special agents are trained to fire this weapon from standing and kneeling positions. Above, an agent is shown firing the weapon on "full automatic." Note the two empty cartridge cases in the air above the weapon. Below this photo is a row of agents firing the weapon on the range. Note that they all lean forward when firing, to keep the muzzle from rising. On the opposite page are some views of night firing training using tracer bullets so the hits can be tracked. Note the ricocheting tracer bullets in the backgrounds of the top and bottom photos, as the agents attack a "criminal hideout" and a silhouette target with the tommy gun.

FBI's Central Gun Vault

In every FBI field office there is a well-protected gun vault where ammunition and heavy weapons are stored for use in raids on criminal hideouts. The photo above shows the central gun vault at Quantico, Virginia. Here are stored hundreds of rifles, shotguns, and submachine guns used for training purposes. Every special agent must be able to take these shoulder weapons apart and assemble them again — blindfolded! A staff of highly skilled gunsmiths constantly checks the operation and accuracy of FBI weapons. Guns must function perfectly and shoot as straight as the man using them can aim. Every G-man is taught that expert marksmanship is the cheapest life insurance he can own.

Know Your FBI

The next time you are in Washington, D.C., visit the FBI Headquarters and see many of its fascinating operations for yourselves. There is no charge for a tour, nor is any appointment required for either an individual or a small group. The tour lasts about one hour and you will see many exhibits concerning famous criminal and security investigations, a demonstration of the FBI's use of firearms, and scientific evidence being examined in the FBI Laboratory. Some 700,000 visitors take this tour each year and come away with a better knowledge of, and a far greater pride in, the work of the bureau and its special agents. These tours are offered Mondays through Fridays, excluding holidays, from 9:15 A.M. until 4:15 P.M. It will be a never-forgotten experience! In upper photo a touring group visits the famous laboratory. Below, they watch a FBI marksman fire the tommy gun.

IN MEMORY OF
SPECIAL AGENTS
OF THE
FEDERAL BUREAU OF INVESTIGATION
WHO HAVE GIVEN THEIR LIVES
IN LINE OF DUTY

EDWIN C. SHANAHAN	OCT. 11. 1925
PAUL E. REYNOLDS	AUG. 9. 1929
ALBERT L. INGLE	NOV. 24. 1931
RAYMOND J. CAFFREY	JUNE 17. 1933
RUPERT V. SURRATT	OCT. 8. 1933
W. CARTER BAUM	APRIL 22. 1934
HERMAN E. HOLLIS	NOV. 27. 1934
SAMUEL P. COWLEY	NOV. 28. 1934
NELSON B. KLEIN	AUG. 16. 1935
WIMBERLY W. BAKER	APR. 17. 1937
TRUETT E. ROWE	JUNE 1. 1937
WILLIAM R. RAMSEY	MAY 3. 1938
HUBERT J. TREACY, JR.	MARCH 13. 1942
P. E. FOXWORTH	JAN. 15. 1943
HAROLD D. HABERFELD	JAN. 15. 1943
J. CORDES DELWORTH	DEC. 3. 1945
JOSEPH J. BROCK	JULY 26. 1952
J. BRADY MURPHY	SEPT. 26. 1953
RICHARD P. HORAN	APRIL 18. 1957
TERRY R. ANDERSON	MAY 17. 1966
DOUGLAS M. PRICE	APRIL 25. 1968
ANTHONY PALMISANO	JAN. 8. 1969
EDWIN R. WOODRIFFE	JAN. 8. 1969

That Others May Live in Security

This simple plaque bearing the names of special agents of the Federal Bureau of Investigation who have given their lives in the line of duty hangs in the FBI Headquarters in Washington, D.C. These brave men laid down their lives that the cause of law and order, and of democracy and justice, might prevail. In the continuing battle against the criminal and the subversive, their sacrifices should never be forgotten. They exemplified the highest standards of "Fidelity, Bravery and Integrity," the motto of the FBI, and its creed. All Americans owe them much.